Kindergarten Letters, Words & Sentences

This workbook uses a 'dot to dot' illustrated system so kids can easily trace letters and learn how to correctly perform their pencil strokes. This ensures good habits from the earliest stage to write well-formed letters and words.

INSIDE THE WORKBOOK

This workbook is divided into the following sections.

PART ONE: THE ALPHABET

Learn to write each letter of the alphabet - both uppercase and lowercase - until each one has been mastered. Follow the dot to dot method for easy learning.

PART TWO: WRITING WORDS

You use the skills you have learnt so far to write a selection of words. Starting easy, you work up to more complex words.

PART THREE: WRITING SENTENCES

The last stage builds upon on all the practice in parts one and two, to allow you to write complete sentences.

Part One: Learning Your Letters

HOW TO WRITE THIS LETTER

Starting at 1, trace the letter by following the numbers in the circles.

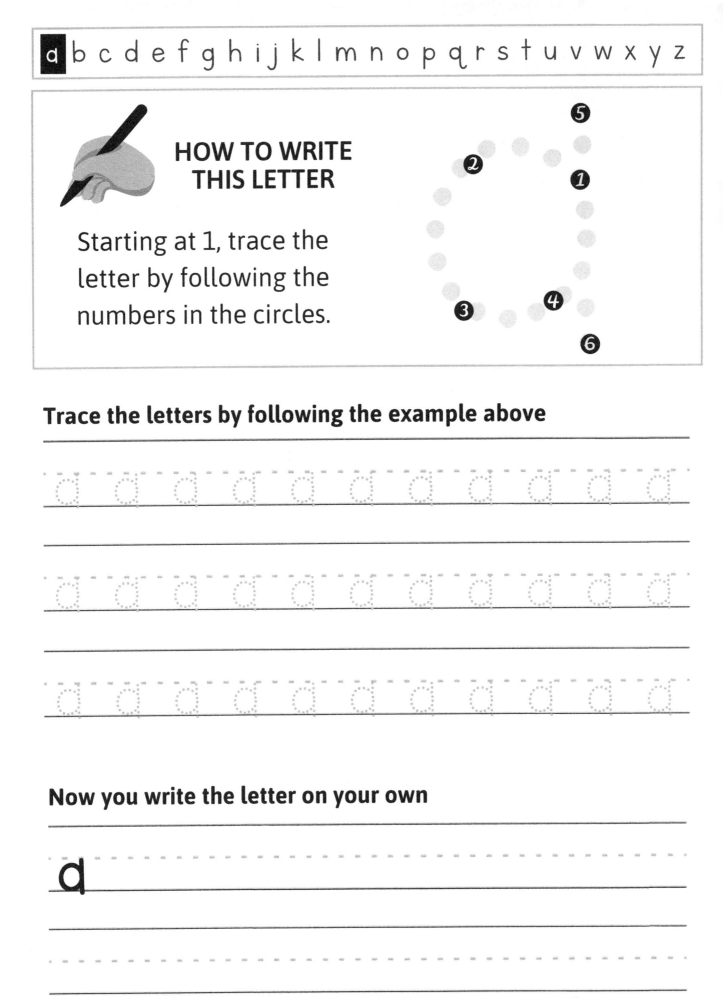

Trace the letters by following the example above

a a a a a a a a a a a a

a a a a a a a a a a a a

a a a a a a a a a a a a

Now you write the letter on your own

a

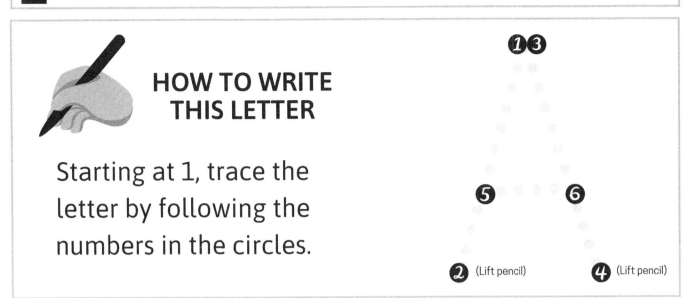

HOW TO WRITE THIS LETTER

Starting at 1, trace the letter by following the numbers in the circles.

①③

⑤   **⑥**

② (Lift pencil)   **④** (Lift pencil)

Trace the letters by following the example above

Now you write the letter on your own

A

a **b** c d e f g h i j k l m n o p q r s t u v w x y z

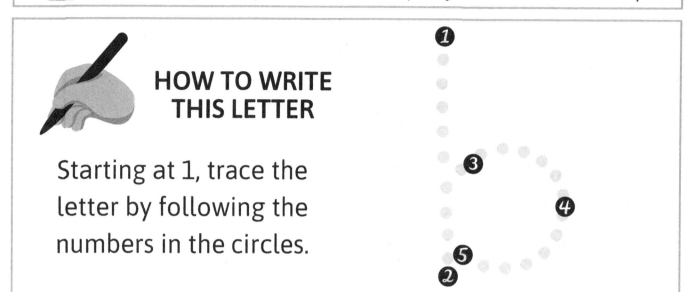

HOW TO WRITE THIS LETTER

Starting at 1, trace the letter by following the numbers in the circles.

Trace the letters by following the example above

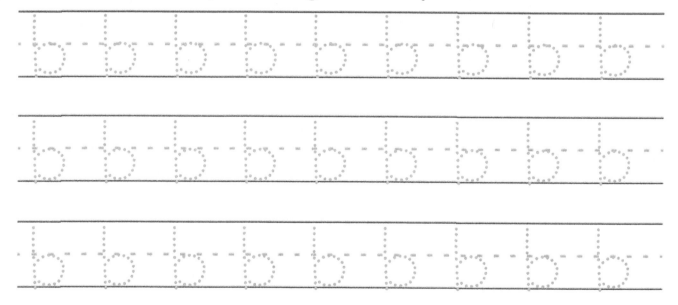

Now you write the letter on your own

b

A B C D E F G H I J K L M N O P Q R S T U V W X Y Z

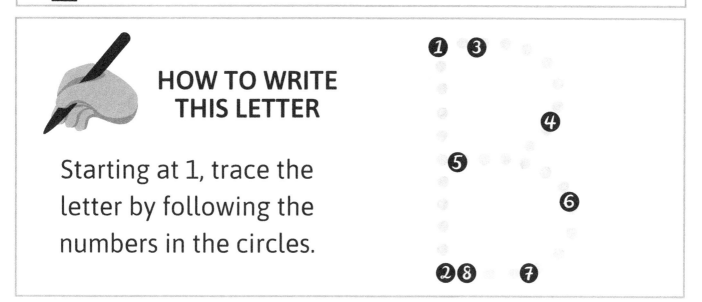

HOW TO WRITE THIS LETTER

Starting at 1, trace the letter by following the numbers in the circles.

Trace the letters by following the example above

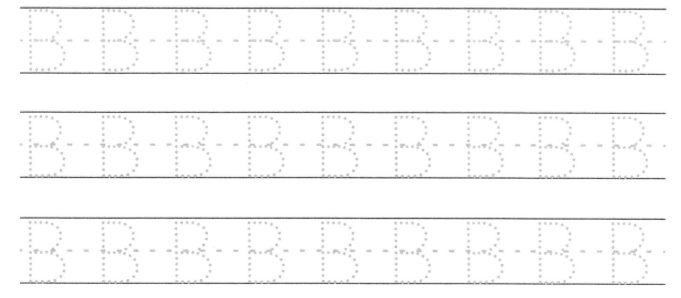

Now you write the letter on your own

B

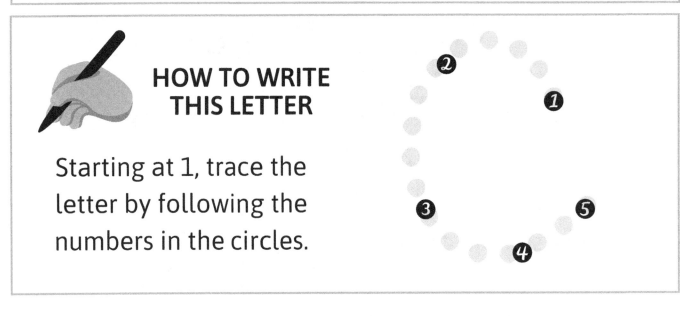

HOW TO WRITE THIS LETTER

Starting at 1, trace the letter by following the numbers in the circles.

Trace the letters by following the example above

c c c c c c c c c c c c c c c

c c c c c c c c c c c c c c c

c c c c c c c c c c c c c c c

Now you write the letter on your own

C

A B C D E F G H I J K L M N O P Q R S T U V W X Y Z

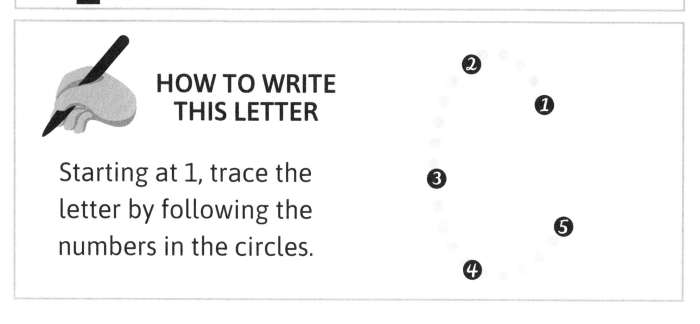

HOW TO WRITE THIS LETTER

Starting at 1, trace the letter by following the numbers in the circles.

Trace the letters by following the example above

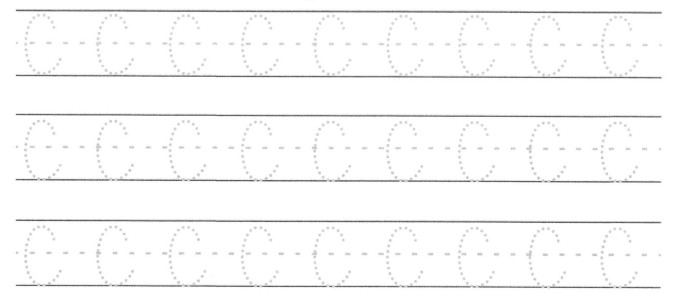

Now you write the letter on your own

C

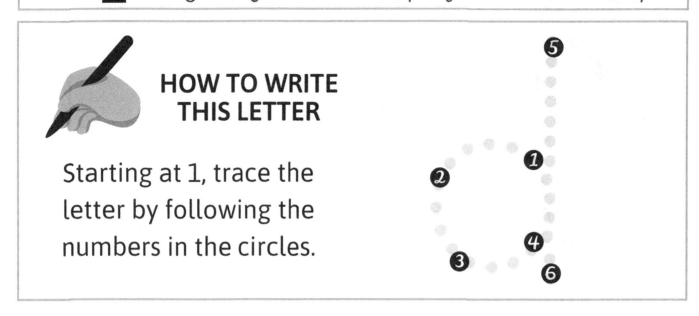

HOW TO WRITE THIS LETTER

Starting at 1, trace the letter by following the numbers in the circles.

Trace the letters by following the example above

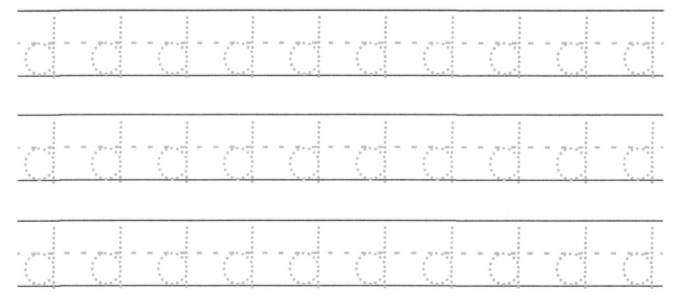

Now you write the letter on your own

d

A B C **D** E F G H I J K L M N O P Q R S T U V W X Y Z

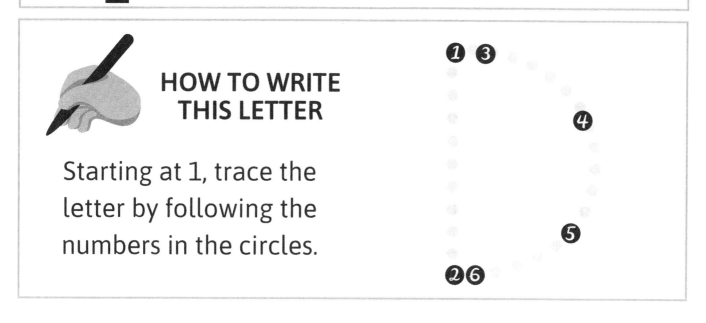

HOW TO WRITE THIS LETTER

Starting at 1, trace the letter by following the numbers in the circles.

Trace the letters by following the example above

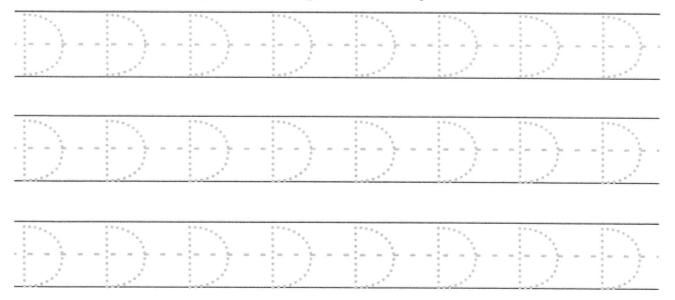

Now you write the letter on your own

D

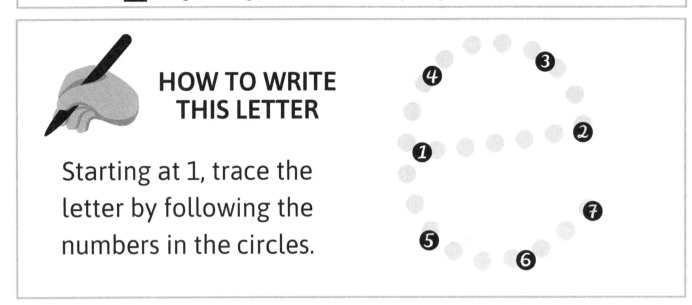

HOW TO WRITE THIS LETTER

Starting at 1, trace the letter by following the numbers in the circles.

Trace the letters by following the example above

e e e e e e e e e e e

e e e e e e e e e e e

e e e e e e e e e e e

Now you write the letter on your own

e

A B C D **E** F G H I J K L M N O P Q R S T U V W X Y Z

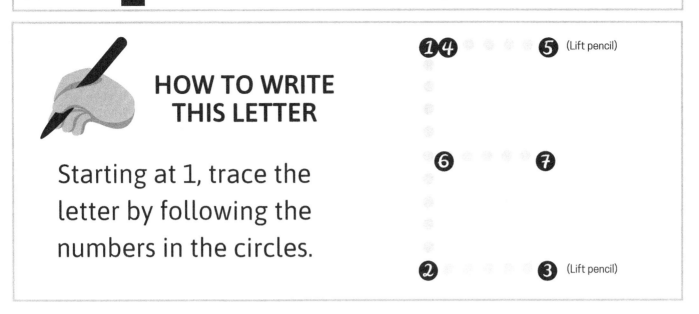

HOW TO WRITE THIS LETTER

Starting at 1, trace the letter by following the numbers in the circles.

Trace the letters by following the example above

Now you write the letter on your own

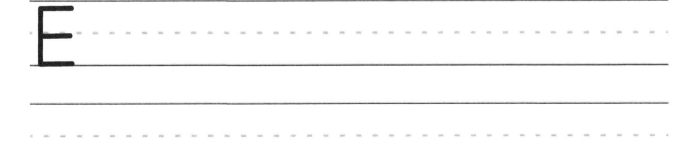

HOW TO WRITE THIS LETTER

Starting at 1, trace the letter by following the numbers in the circles.

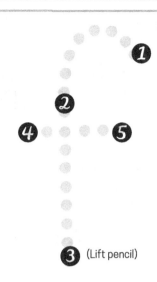

(Lift pencil)

Trace the letters by following the example above

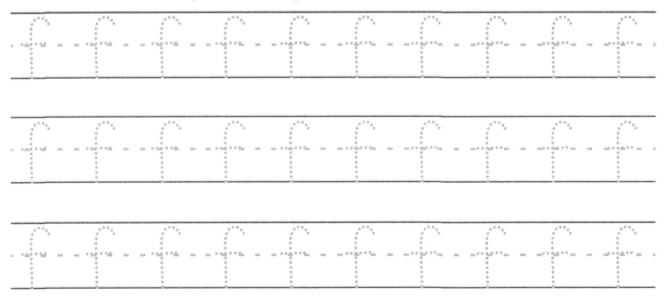

Now you write the letter on your own

f

A B C D E **F** G H I J K L M N O P Q R S T U V W X Y Z

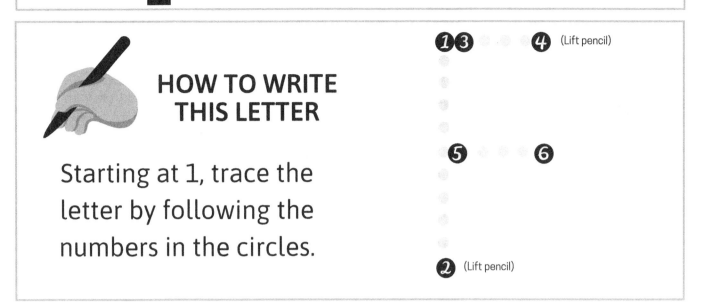

HOW TO WRITE THIS LETTER

Starting at 1, trace the letter by following the numbers in the circles.

❶❸ ④ (Lift pencil)

❺ ❻

❷ (Lift pencil)

Trace the letters by following the example above

Now you write the letter on your own

F

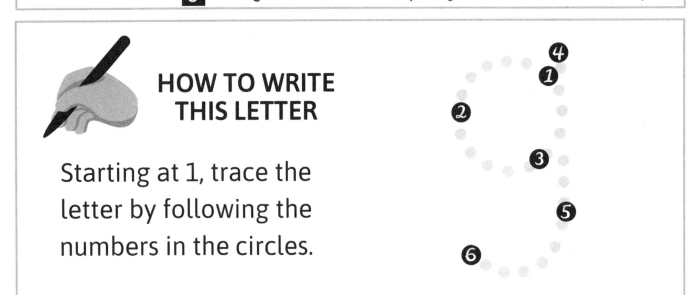

HOW TO WRITE THIS LETTER

Starting at 1, trace the letter by following the numbers in the circles.

Trace the letters by following the example above

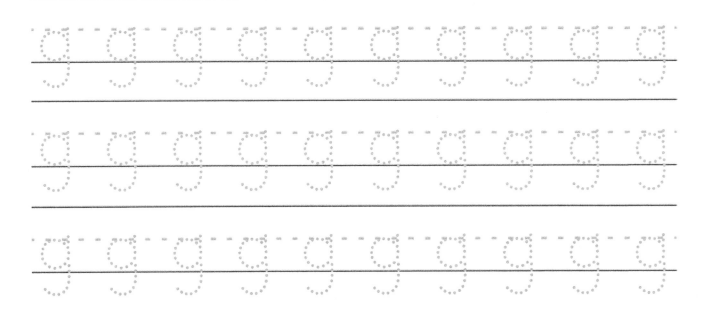

Now you write the letter on your own

g

A B C D E F **G** H I J K L M N O P Q R S T U V W X Y Z

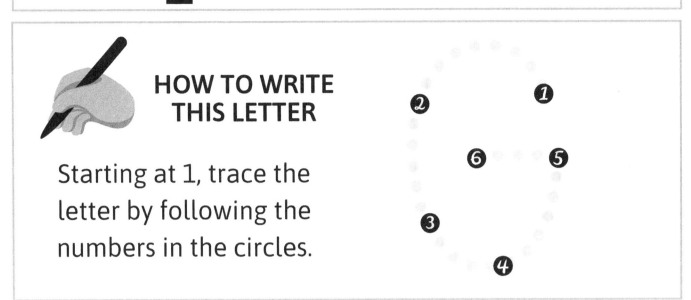

HOW TO WRITE THIS LETTER

Starting at 1, trace the letter by following the numbers in the circles.

Trace the letters by following the example above

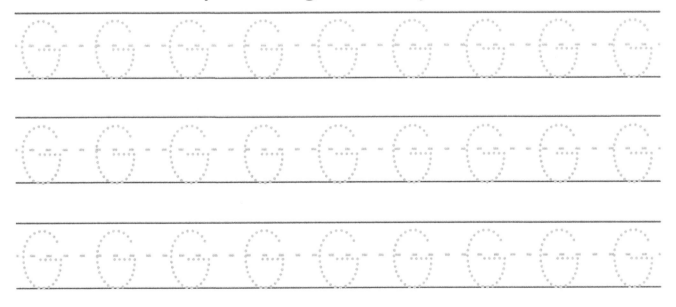

Now you write the letter on your own

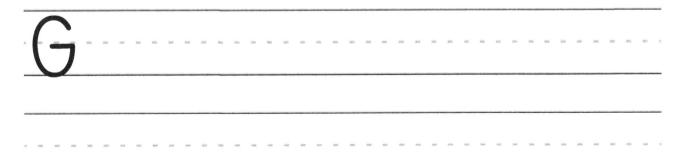

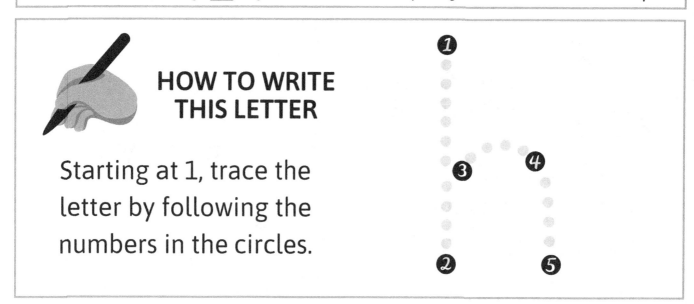

HOW TO WRITE THIS LETTER

Starting at 1, trace the letter by following the numbers in the circles.

Trace the letters by following the example above

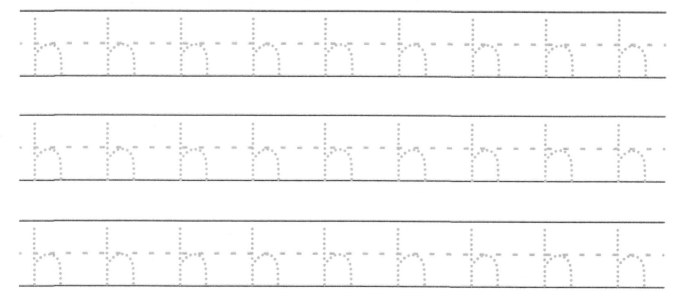

Now you write the letter on your own

A B C D E F G **H** I J K L M N O P Q R S T U V W X Y Z

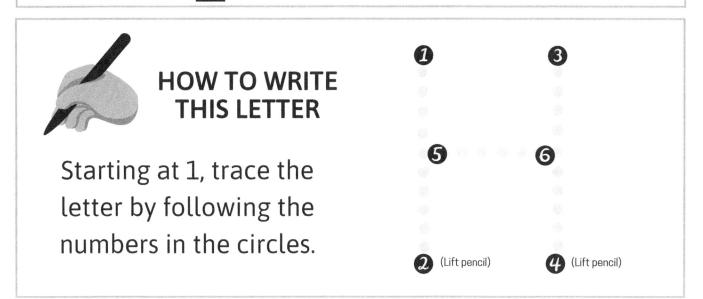

HOW TO WRITE THIS LETTER

Starting at 1, trace the letter by following the numbers in the circles.

① ③

⑤ ⑥

② (Lift pencil) ④ (Lift pencil)

Trace the letters by following the example above

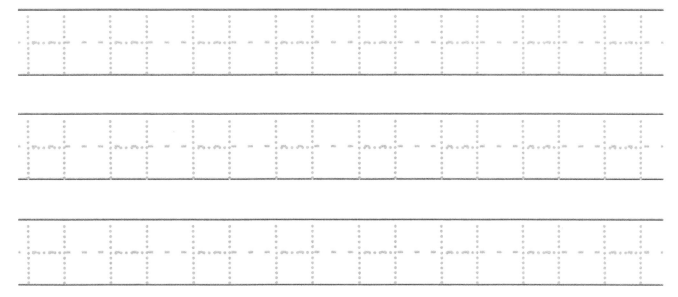

Now you write the letter on your own

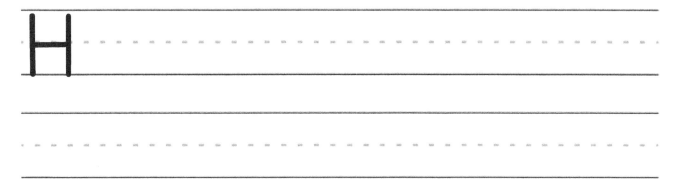

a b c d e f g h **i** j k l m n o p q r s t u v w x y z

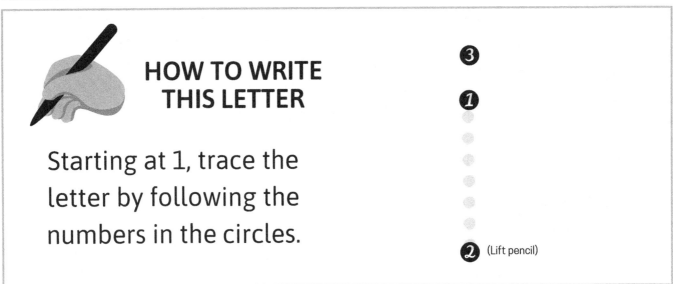

HOW TO WRITE THIS LETTER

Starting at 1, trace the letter by following the numbers in the circles.

❸

❶

❷ (Lift pencil)

Trace the letters by following the example above

Now you write the letter on your own

A B C D E F G H **I** J K L M N O P Q R S T U V W X Y Z

HOW TO WRITE THIS LETTER

Starting at 1, trace the letter by following the numbers in the circles.

❸   ❶   ❹ (Lift pencil)

(Lift pencil)

❺   ❷   ❻

Trace the letters by following the example above

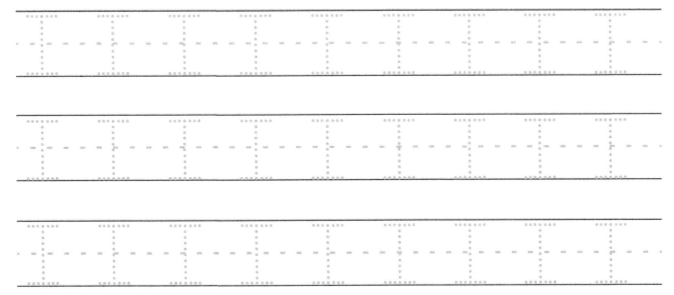

Now you write the letter on your own

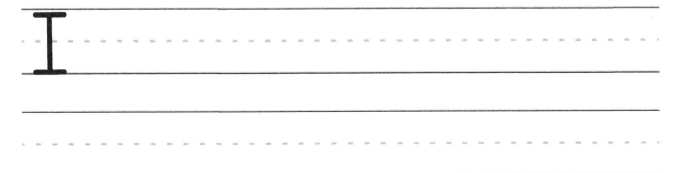

HOW TO WRITE THIS LETTER

Starting at 1, trace the letter by following the numbers in the circles.

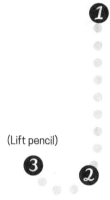

(Lift pencil)

Trace the letters by following the example above

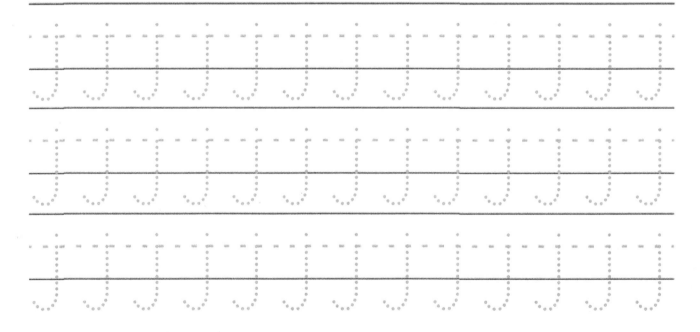

Now you write the letter on your own

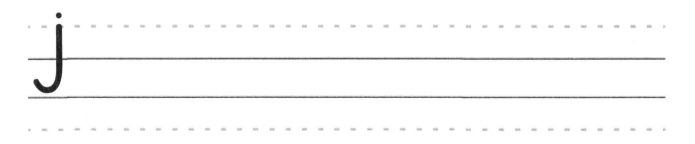

j

A B C D E F G H I **J** K L M N O P Q R S T U V W X Y Z

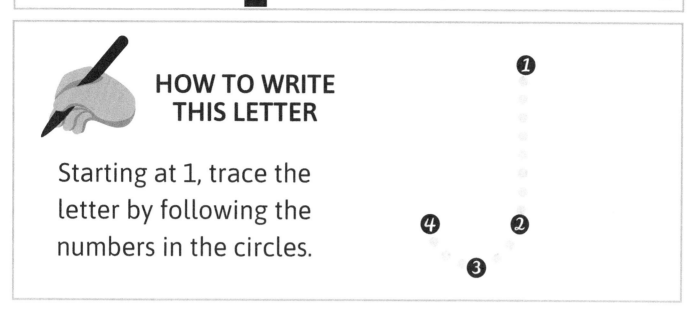

HOW TO WRITE THIS LETTER

Starting at 1, trace the letter by following the numbers in the circles.

Trace the letters by following the example above

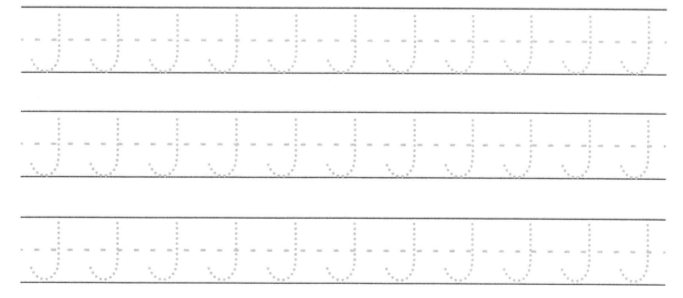

Now you write the letter on your own

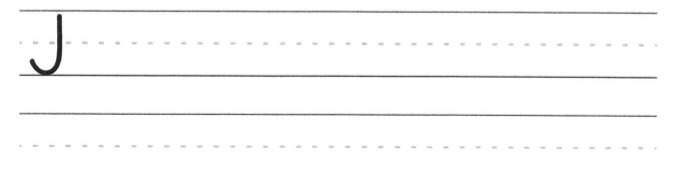

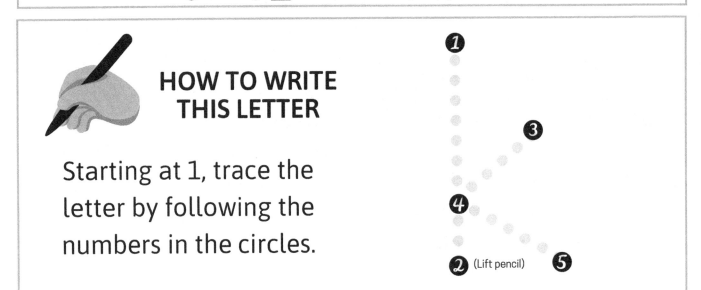

HOW TO WRITE THIS LETTER

Starting at 1, trace the letter by following the numbers in the circles.

① ③ ④ ② (Lift pencil) ⑤

Trace the letters by following the example above

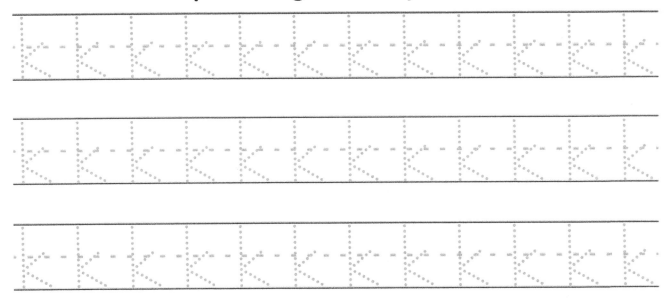

Now you write the letter on your own

k

A B C D E F G H I J **K** L M N O P Q R S T U V W X Y Z

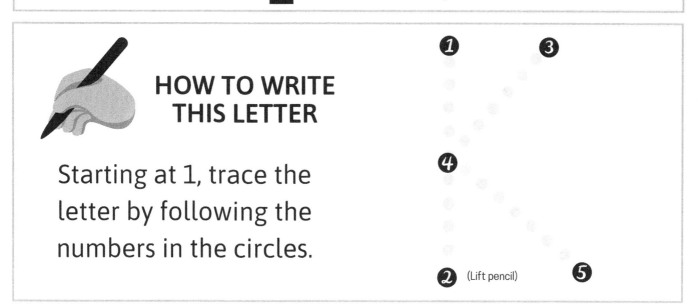

HOW TO WRITE THIS LETTER

Starting at 1, trace the letter by following the numbers in the circles.

1 **3**

4

2 (Lift pencil) **5**

Trace the letters by following the example above

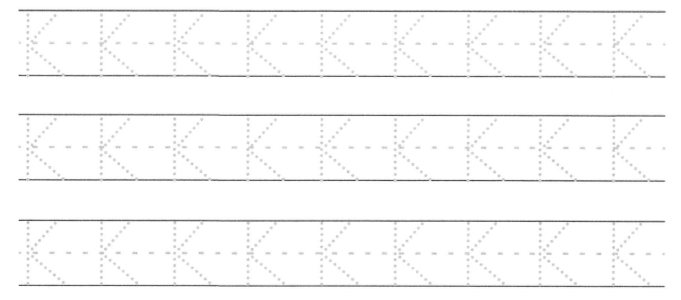

Now you write the letter on your own

K

a b c d e f g h i j k **l** m n o p q r s t u v w x y z

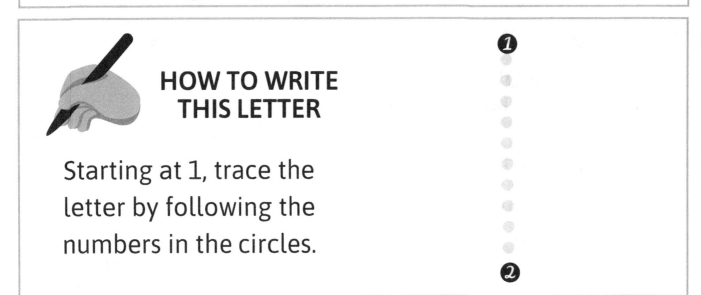

HOW TO WRITE THIS LETTER

Starting at 1, trace the letter by following the numbers in the circles.

❶

❷

Trace the letters by following the example above

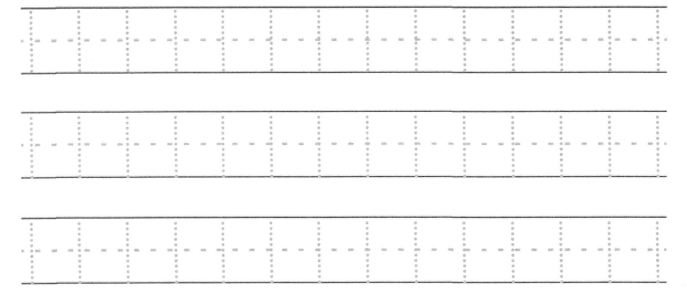

Now you write the letter on your own

A B C D E F G H I J K **L** M N O P Q R S T U V W X Y Z

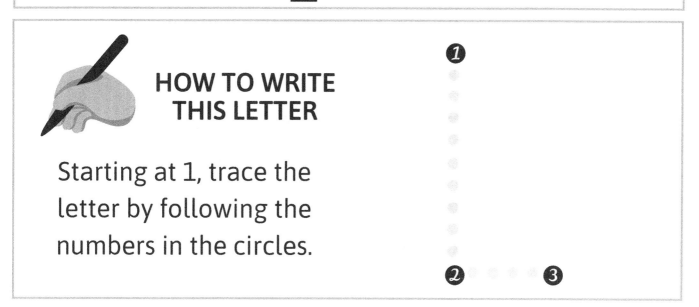

HOW TO WRITE THIS LETTER

Starting at 1, trace the letter by following the numbers in the circles.

Trace the letters by following the example above

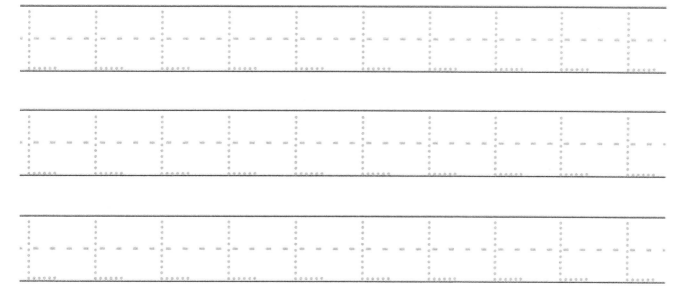

Now you write the letter on your own

HOW TO WRITE THIS LETTER

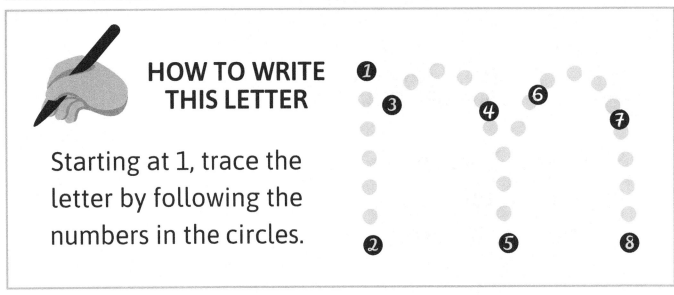

Starting at 1, trace the letter by following the numbers in the circles.

Trace the letters by following the example above

m m m m m m m m m m m

m m m m m m m m m m m

m m m m m m m m m m m

Now you write the letter on your own

m

A B C D E F G H I J K L **M** N O P Q R S T U V W X Y Z

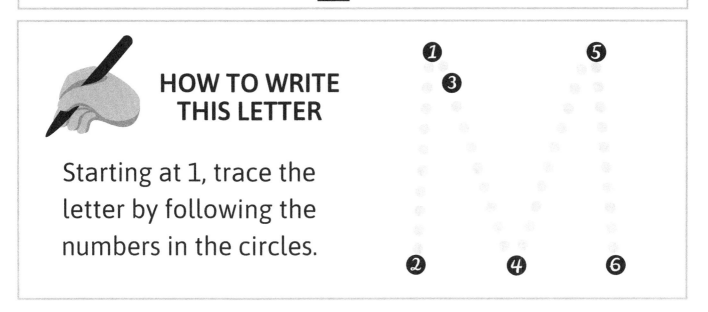

HOW TO WRITE THIS LETTER

Starting at 1, trace the letter by following the numbers in the circles.

Trace the letters by following the example above

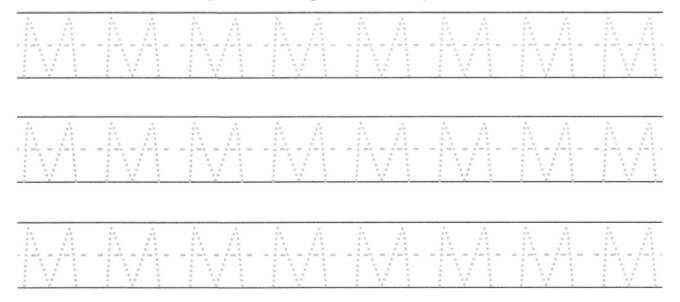

Now you write the letter on your own

M

a b c d e f g h i j k l m **n** o p q r s t u v w x y z

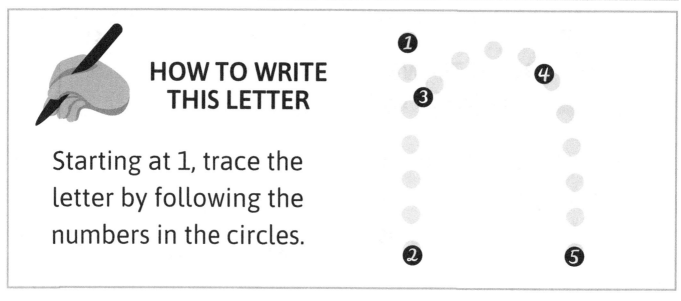

HOW TO WRITE THIS LETTER

Starting at 1, trace the letter by following the numbers in the circles.

Trace the letters by following the example above

n n n n n n n n n n n n n n n n n

n n n n n n n n n n n n n n n n n

n n n n n n n n n n n n n n n n n

Now you write the letter on your own

n

A B C D E F G H I J K L M **N** O P Q R S T U V W X Y Z

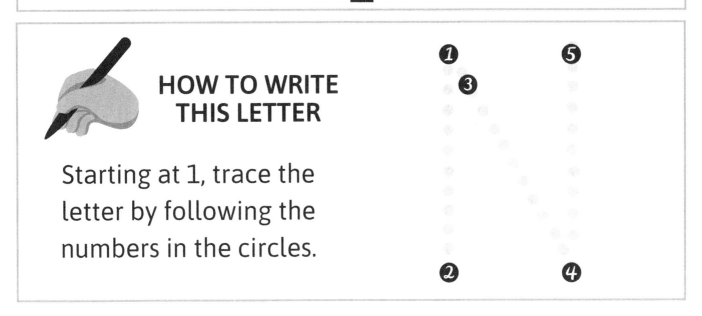

HOW TO WRITE THIS LETTER

Starting at 1, trace the letter by following the numbers in the circles.

Trace the letters by following the example above

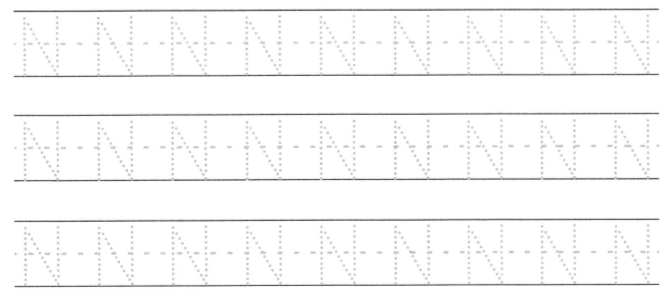

Now you write the letter on your own

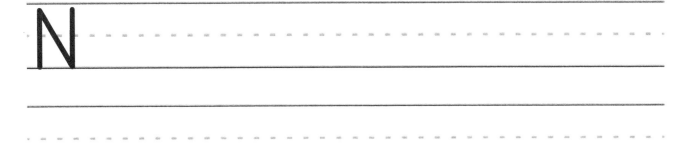

HOW TO WRITE THIS LETTER

Starting at 1, trace the letter by following the numbers in the circles.

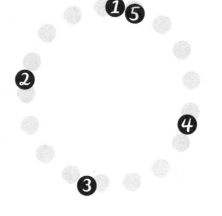

Trace the letters by following the example above

Now you write the letter on your own

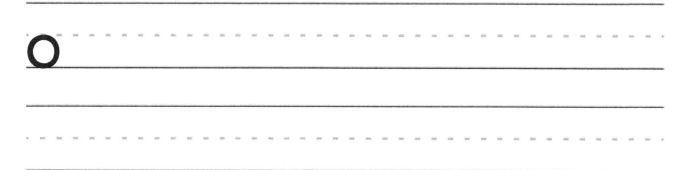

A B C D E F G H I J K L M N **O** P Q R S T U V W X Y Z

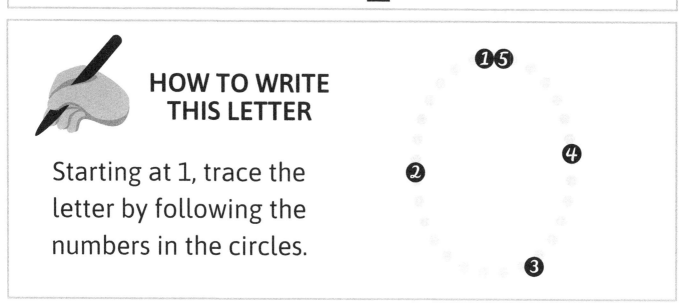

HOW TO WRITE THIS LETTER

Starting at 1, trace the letter by following the numbers in the circles.

Trace the letters by following the example above

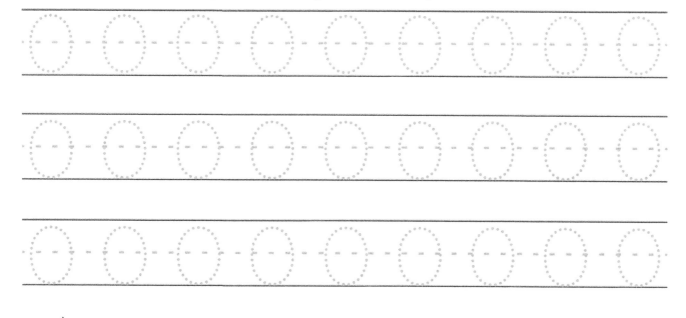

Now you write the letter on your own

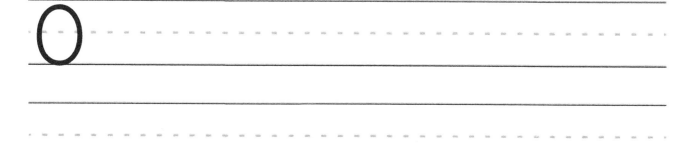

HOW TO WRITE THIS LETTER

Starting at 1, trace the letter by following the numbers in the circles.

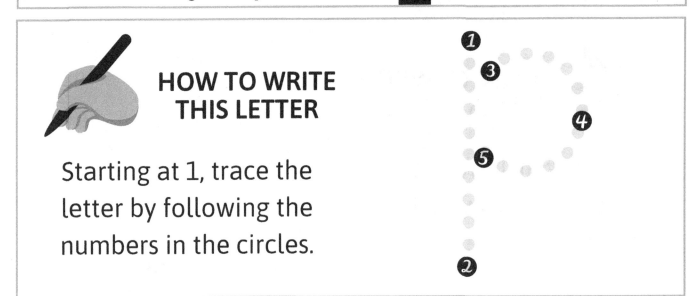

Trace the letters by following the example above

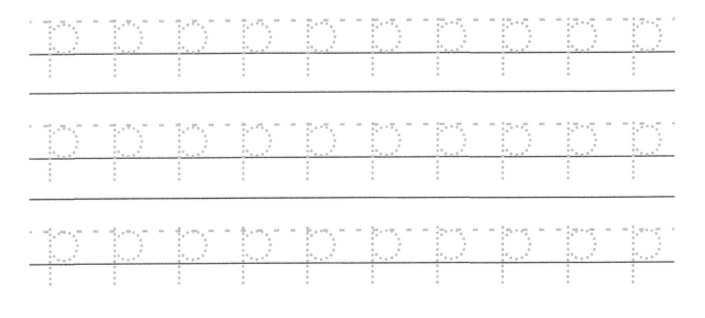

Now you write the letter on your own

p

A B C D E F G H I J K L M N O P Q R S T U V W X Y Z

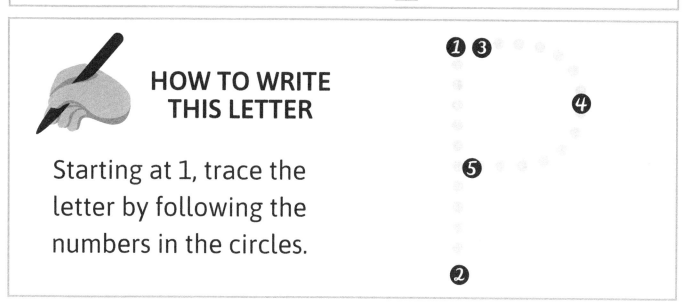

HOW TO WRITE THIS LETTER

Starting at 1, trace the letter by following the numbers in the circles.

Trace the letters by following the example above

P P P P P P P P P P P P P

P P P P P P P P P P P P P

P P P P P P P P P P P P P

Now you write the letter on your own

P

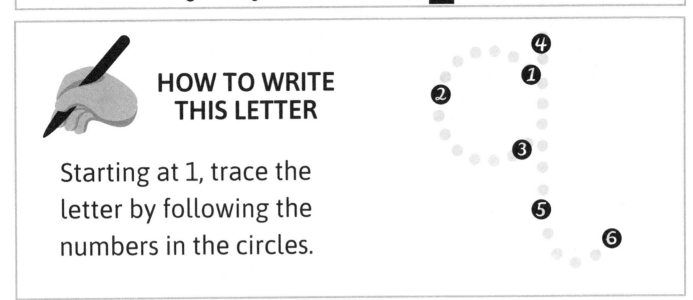

HOW TO WRITE THIS LETTER

Starting at 1, trace the letter by following the numbers in the circles.

Trace the letters by following the example above

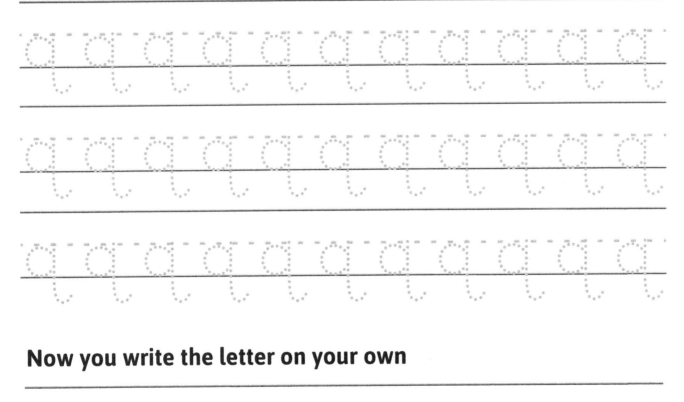

Now you write the letter on your own

A B C D E F G H I J K L M N O P Q R S T U V W X Y Z

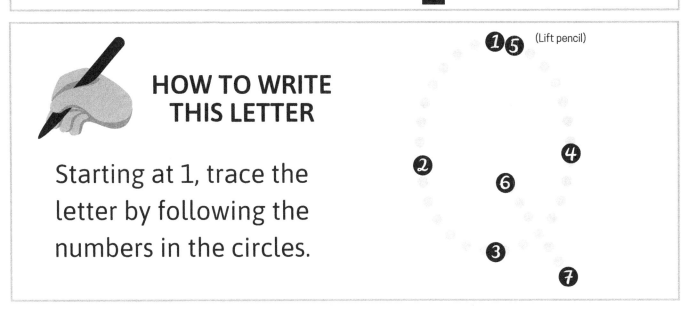

HOW TO WRITE THIS LETTER

Starting at 1, trace the letter by following the numbers in the circles.

(Lift pencil)

Trace the letters by following the example above

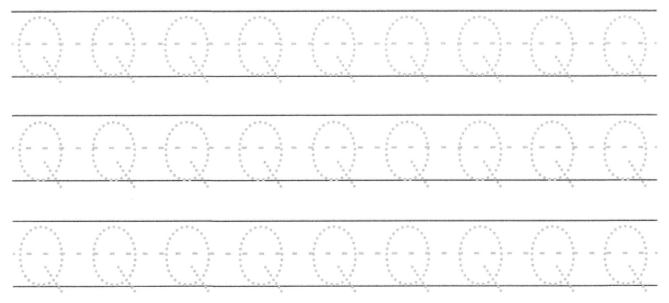

Now you write the letter on your own

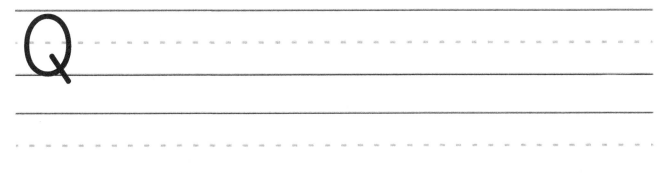

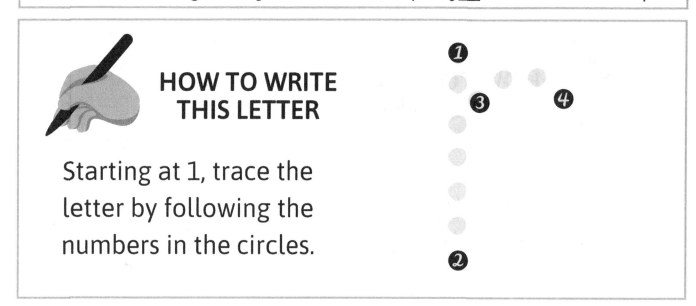

HOW TO WRITE THIS LETTER

Starting at 1, trace the letter by following the numbers in the circles.

Trace the letters by following the example above

Now you write the letter on your own

r

A B C D E F G H I J K L M N O P Q **R** S T U V W X Y Z

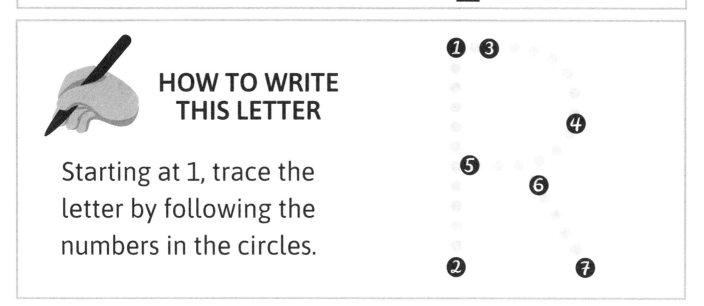

HOW TO WRITE THIS LETTER

Starting at 1, trace the letter by following the numbers in the circles.

Trace the letters by following the example above

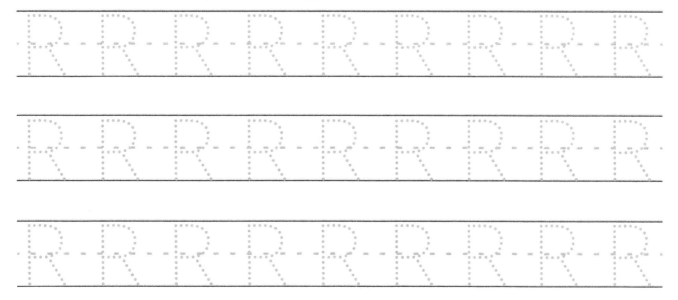

Now you write the letter on your own

R

HOW TO WRITE THIS LETTER

Starting at 1, trace the letter by following the numbers in the circles.

Trace the letters by following the example above

S S S S S S S S S S S S S S S S S

S S S S S S S S S S S S S S S S S

S S S S S S S S S S S S S S S S S

Now you write the letter on your own

S

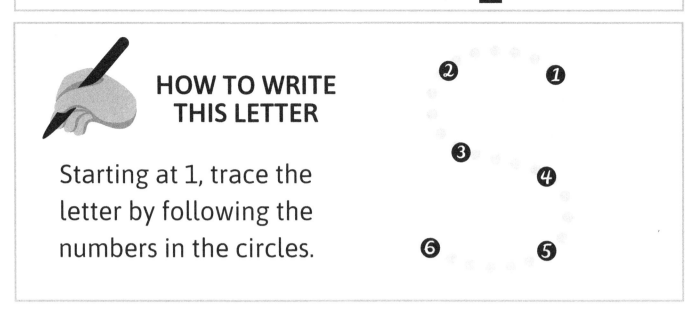

HOW TO WRITE THIS LETTER

Starting at 1, trace the letter by following the numbers in the circles.

Trace the letters by following the example above

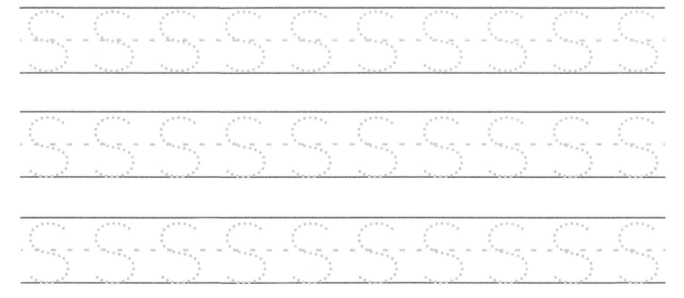

Now you write the letter on your own

S

a b c d e f g h i j k l m n o p q r s **t** u v w x y z

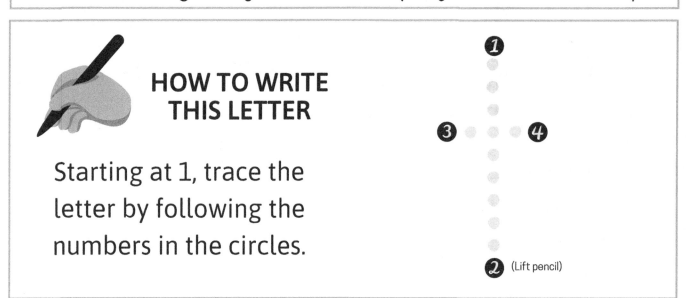

HOW TO WRITE THIS LETTER

Starting at 1, trace the letter by following the numbers in the circles.

1

3 **4**

2 (Lift pencil)

Trace the letters by following the example above

Now you write the letter on your own

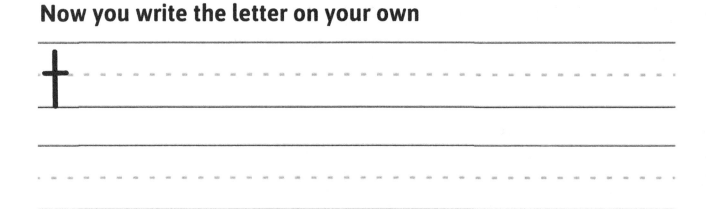

A B C D E F G H I J K L M N O P Q R S **T** U V W X Y Z

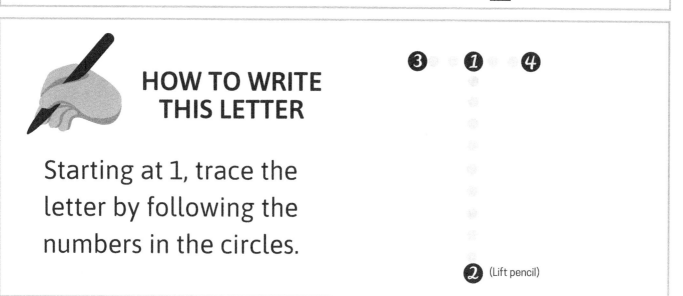

HOW TO WRITE THIS LETTER

Starting at 1, trace the letter by following the numbers in the circles.

❸ ❶ ❹

❷ (Lift pencil)

Trace the letters by following the example above

Now you write the letter on your own

T

a b c d e f g h i j k l m n o p q r s t **u** v w x y z

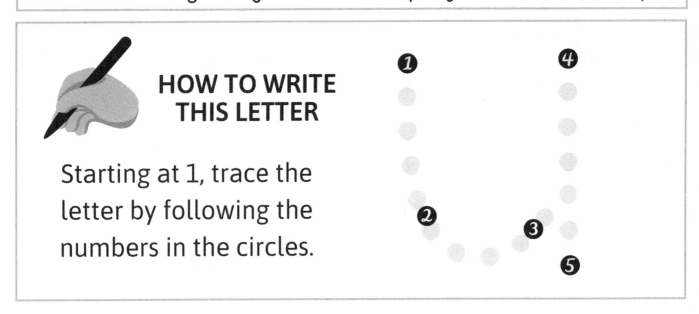

HOW TO WRITE THIS LETTER

Starting at 1, trace the letter by following the numbers in the circles.

Trace the letters by following the example above

Now you write the letter on your own

u

A B C D E F G H I J K L M N O P Q R S T **U** V W X Y Z

HOW TO WRITE THIS LETTER

Starting at 1, trace the letter by following the numbers in the circles.

Trace the letters by following the example above

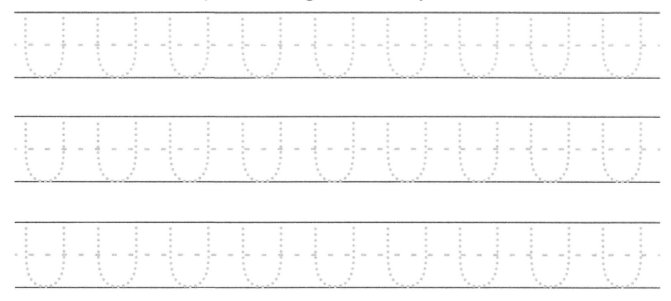

Now you write the letter on your own

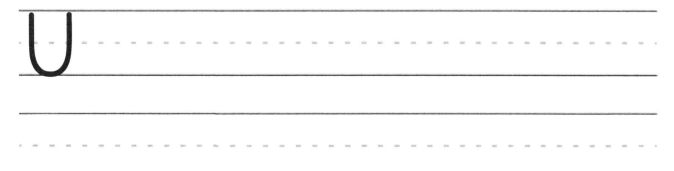

HOW TO WRITE THIS LETTER

Starting at 1, trace the letter by following the numbers in the circles.

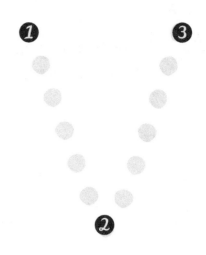

Trace the letters by following the example above

v v v v v v v v v v v v v v v v v v v v

v v v v v v v v v v v v v v v v v v v v

v v v v v v v v v v v v v v v v v v v v

Now you write the letter on your own

V

A B C D E F G H I J K L M N O P Q R S T U **V** W X Y Z

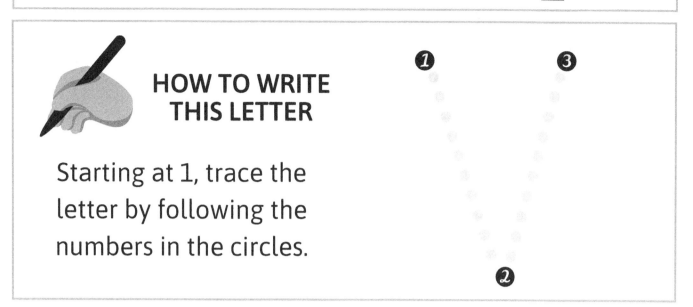

HOW TO WRITE THIS LETTER

Starting at 1, trace the letter by following the numbers in the circles.

Trace the letters by following the example above

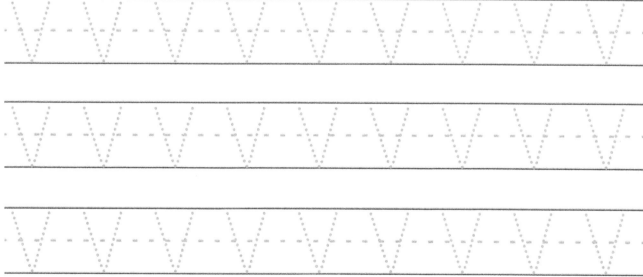

Now you write the letter on your own

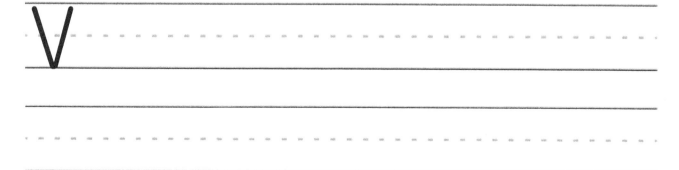

HOW TO WRITE THIS LETTER

Starting at 1, trace the letter by following the numbers in the circles.

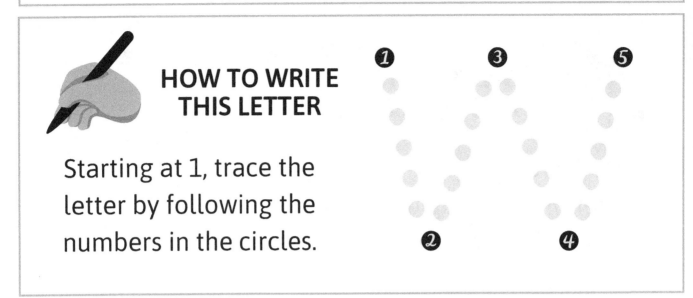

Trace the letters by following the example above

w w w w w w w w w w w w

w w w w w w w w w w w w

w w w w w w w w w w w w

Now you write the letter on your own

W

A B C D E F G H I J K L M N O P Q R S T U V **W** X Y Z

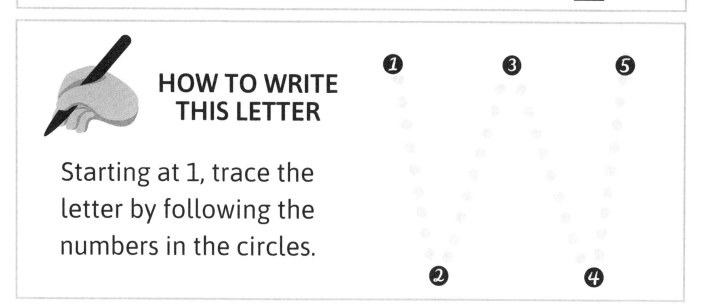

HOW TO WRITE THIS LETTER

Starting at 1, trace the letter by following the numbers in the circles.

Trace the letters by following the example above

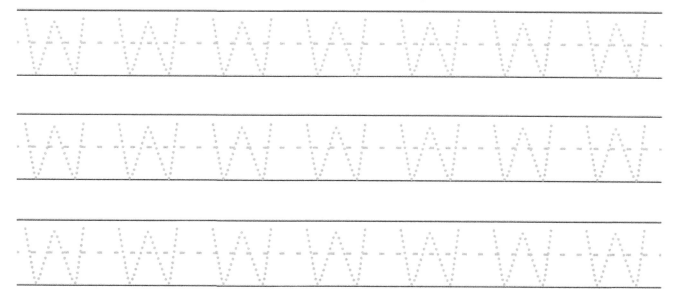

Now you write the letter on your own

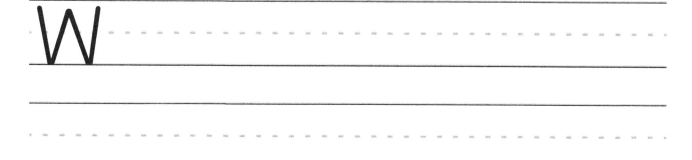

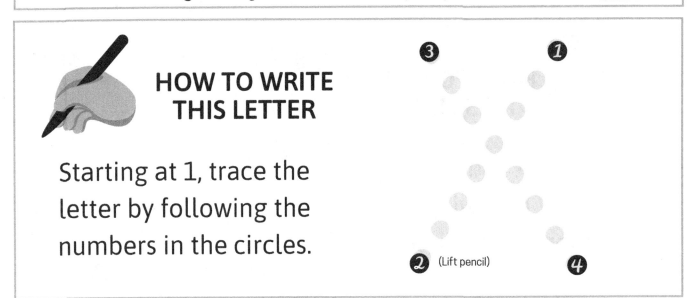

HOW TO WRITE THIS LETTER

Starting at 1, trace the letter by following the numbers in the circles.

❸   ❶

❷ (Lift pencil)   ❹

Trace the letters by following the example above

x x x x x x x x x x x x x x x x

x x x x x x x x x x x x x x x x

x x x x x x x x x x x x x x x x

Now you write the letter on your own

X

A B C D E F G H I J K L M N O P Q R S T U V W **X** Y Z

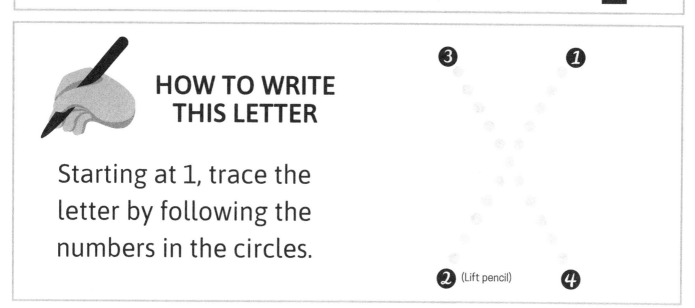

HOW TO WRITE THIS LETTER

Starting at 1, trace the letter by following the numbers in the circles.

❸   ❶

❷ (Lift pencil)   ❹

Trace the letters by following the example above

X - X - X - X - X - X - X - X - X - X - X

X - X - X - X - X - X - X - X - X - X - X

X - X - X - X - X - X - X - X - X - X - X

Now you write the letter on your own

X

HOW TO WRITE THIS LETTER

Starting at 1, trace the letter by following the numbers in the circles.

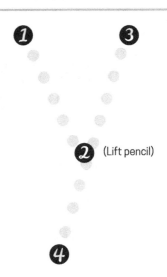

❶   ❸

❷ (Lift pencil)

❹

Trace the letters by following the example above

Now you write the letter on your own

y

A B C D E F G H I J K L M N O P Q R S T U V W X **Y** Z

HOW TO WRITE THIS LETTER

Starting at 1, trace the letter by following the numbers in the circles.

 (Lift pencil)

Trace the letters by following the example above

Now you write the letter on your own

Y

a b c d e f g h i j k l m n o p q r s t u v w x y **z**

HOW TO WRITE THIS LETTER

Starting at 1, trace the letter by following the numbers in the circles.

❶ ❷
❸ ❹

Trace the letters by following the example above

Now you write the letter on your own

Z

A B C D E F G H I J K L M N O P Q R S T U V W X Y Z

HOW TO WRITE THIS LETTER

Starting at 1, trace the letter by following the numbers in the circles.

Trace the letters by following the example above

Now you write the letter on your own

Z

a b c d e f g h i j k l m n o p q r s t u v w x y z

A B C D E F G H I J K L M N O P Q R S T U V W X Y Z

 **Practice any letters that you found difficult on this blank page**

a b c d e f g h i j k l m n o p q r s t u v w x y z

A B C D E F G H I J K L M N O P Q R S T U V W X Y Z

 **Practice any letters that you found difficult on this blank page**

a b c d e f g h i j k l m n o p q r s t u v w x y z

A B C D E F G H I J K L M N O P Q R S T U V W X Y Z

 **Practice any letters that you found difficult on this blank page**

Part Two: Writing Words

glad glad glad glad

Trace the dotted words, then write them beneath

hand hand hand

baby baby baby baby

girl girl girl girl girl

Trace the dotted words, then write them beneath

late late late late late

Trace the dotted words, then write them beneath

wind wind wind

truck truck truck

Trace the dotted words, then write them beneath

name name name

lunch lunch lunch

Trace the dotted words, then write them beneath

away away away

nice nice nice nice

candy candy candy

Trace the dotted words, then write them beneath

drive drive drive

Trace the dotted words, then write them beneath

very very very very

club club club club

Trace the dotted words, then write them beneath

what what what

farm farm farm

Trace the dotted words, then write them beneath

riding riding riding

each each each each

Trace the dotted words, then write them beneath

tree tree tree tree

heard heard heard

Trace the dotted words, then write them beneath

family family family

cattle cattle cattle

Trace the dotted words, then write them beneath

dinner dinner dinner

Kitten Kitten Kitten

Trace the dotted words, then write them beneath

Large Large Large

inches inches inches

Trace the dotted words, then write them beneath

Juice Juice Juice

Shield Shield Shield

Trace the dotted words, then write them beneath

Running Running

Merry Merry Merry

Trace the dotted words, then write them beneath

Picture Picture Picture

Winter Winter Winter

Trace the dotted words, then write them beneath

Xray Xray Xray Xray

Under Under Under

Trace the dotted words, then write them beneath

Value Value Value

remember remember

Trace the dotted words, then write them beneath

yesterday yesterday

President President

Trace the dotted words, then write them beneath

Sentence Sentence

Different Different

Trace the dotted words, then write them beneath

Suddenly Suddenly

medicine   medicine

Trace the dotted words, then write them beneath

maximum maximum

happiness happiness

Trace the dotted words, then write them beneath

Beautiful Beautiful

Part Three: Writing Sentences

Write each sentence two times

She checked every store near her home for bread.

I am now going to stand next to my best friend.

She has packed her own lunch from home today.

The water in the pond is three inches below the plants.

We stood around the grass on the first day of school.

His mother wants
him to raise his
grades in science.

Do not show him the round mirror that shattered.

She read the scary story under her covers with a light.

The electric current moves in waves through the wires.

We had to wrap
Mary's wrist and
knee after she fell.

My uncle lives two hundred miles west of here.

An atom is a tiny particle you cannot see using your eyes.

Shall we knock on my sister's door to see how she is?

Watch the cloud change direction in the sky.

He will tell you something funny to make you laugh.

My teacher showed me how to answer the math problem.

We have a chance to travel in a big train today.

I picked up a
blue pencil off the
table in her office.

They were scared when the mirror crashed down.

We cannot get close to the huge giraffe in the zoo.

What is the price to put a fence around this space?

They had to walk through the forest in the night.

Which operation will help me solve the equation?

The sound from the fountain began to grow louder.

His voice makes a noise that will annoy you.

My father read a book by an author who taught writing.

We are learning multiplication and division in class.

Made in the USA
Coppell, TX
21 May 2025

49684109R00063